I0407041

Table Of Contents

Preface

Part 1: The Basics Of Crypto

Part 2: Buying & Selling Crypto

Part 3: Privacy & Security in Crypto

Preface

Welcome to "The Beginner's Guide To Crypto" This book is for anyone who is new to the world of cryptocurrencies and investing and wants to learn more. The purpose of this book is to provide you with a comprehensive guide to understanding the basics of investing in cryptocurrencies.

In this book, we will cover the fundamental concepts of cryptocurrency investing, the basics of what cryptocurrency is, how to use them, and what you need to know in order to start investing & building a profitable portfolio.

As someone who has been involved in the world of cryptocurrencies and investing for many years, I understand how intimidating it can be for beginners to get started.

My goal is to make the process as simple and straightforward as possible and to provide you with the knowledge and tools you need to make informed investment decisions.

I hope this book will be a valuable resource for you as you embark on your journey into the world of crypto and investing. Whether you're a complete beginner or have some experience with cryptocurrencies, I believe that you will find this guide to be helpful in your learning process.

Thank you for choosing to read "The Beginner's Guide to Crypto."
I wish you all the best in your investment journey.

Colin Meunier

decentral21@gmail.com

www.CryptoColin.com

Part 1: The Basics Of Crypto

Chapter 1.
Introduction To Cryptocurrency

Introduction To Cryptocurrency

In recent years, cryptocurrency has become an increasingly popular topic of discussion in the world of finance and technology. Cryptography is the backbone of security for cryptocurrency, which is a form of digital or virtual currency that is not regulated by a central bank or any other financial institution.

This decentralized currency operates independently, allowing for fast and secure transactions, making it a popular alternative to traditional banking methods. Unlike traditional currencies, which are backed by government guarantees, cryptocurrency relies on complex algorithms and decentralized networks to verify transactions and maintain their value.

One of the most well-known and widely used cryptocurrencies is Bitcoin, which was created in 2009 by an unknown person or group using the pseudonym Satoshi Nakamoto. In the years following the introduction of Bitcoin, the world of cryptocurrencies has experienced explosive growth, with hundreds of alternative digital currencies developed. These cryptocurrencies boast a variety of unique features and serve different purposes, from facilitating secure transactions to providing alternative investment opportunities.

The advantages of cryptocurrency include its speed, security, and low transaction fees, as well as its potential to provide financial access to people who are underserved by traditional banking systems. However, there are also potential drawbacks, such as the lack of regulation and the risk of volatility.

This book aims to provide a comprehensive introduction to cryptocurrency for beginners. We will explore what cryptocurrency is, how it works, and the different types of cryptocurrencies that exist. We will also discuss how to get started with cryptocurrency, including choosing a wallet, buying, and trading cryptocurrency, and keeping it secure.

Whether you're a complete beginner or just looking to expand your knowledge of cryptocurrency, this book is for you.

Join me as we embark on an exciting journey to discover the world of cryptocurrencies. Together, we'll delve into the intricacies of digital currencies, explore their innovative features, and gain insights into their potential impact on the future of finance.

Chapter 2.
What is Cryptocurrency

What is Cryptocurrency

Cryptocurrency is a type of currency that is entirely digital and employs cryptographic techniques to ensure secure transactions and manage the creation of new units.

This innovative form of currency operates in a decentralized manner, which implies that it is not governed or managed by any government or financial institution.

Cryptocurrencies operate on a blockchain, which is a distributed ledger technology that records all transactions securely and transparently. The blockchain is maintained by a network of computers, called nodes, that work together to validate transactions and ensure the system's integrity.

Cryptocurrencies are typically bought and sold on exchanges, where they are traded for other cryptocurrencies or traditional fiat currencies like the US dollar or euro. They can also be used as a form of payment for goods and services, with an increasing number of merchants accepting them as valid forms of payment.

One of the critical advantages of cryptocurrencies is their decentralization. Because they are not controlled by any government or financial institution, they are not subject to the same regulations and restrictions as traditional currencies. This makes them attractive to individuals and businesses who want to operate outside the traditional financial system.

Another advantage of cryptocurrencies is their security. Because they use cryptography to secure transactions and control the creation of new units, they are difficult to hack or manipulate. Transactions on the blockchain are also transparent and immutable, meaning that they cannot be altered once they have been recorded.

Bitcoin

The first and most well-known cryptocurrency is Bitcoin. In 2009, a person or group operating under the pseudonym Satoshi Nakamoto introduced Bitcoin to the world. Despite extensive research, the true identity of Satoshi Nakamoto remains unknown to this day.

The true identity of Satoshi Nakamoto has never been revealed, and their reasons for creating Bitcoin are not entirely clear.

However, in the original Bitcoin whitepaper, Satoshi Nakamoto described Bitcoin as a peer-to-peer electronic cash system that would allow for fast and secure transactions without the need for intermediaries like banks or payment processors. This was seen as a response to the 2008 global financial crisis, which highlighted the need for a more decentralized and secure financial system.

Bitcoin was also designed to have a finite supply, with a maximum limit of 21 million bitcoins that can ever be created. This was intended to prevent inflation and maintain the currency's value over time.

Additionally, Bitcoin was created to be a decentralized system not controlled by any government or financial institution. This gives individuals more control over their money and increases privacy and security.

Since its creation, Bitcoin has become the most well-known and widely used cryptocurrency, with a market capitalization of over $1 trillion as of early 2021. The emergence of Bitcoin has sparked the creation of numerous other cryptocurrencies, each possessing its distinctive attributes and applications. As a result, the world of digital currencies has witnessed a vast array of novel cryptocurrencies, each with its unique set of features and use cases.

Alt Coins

Alternative coins, more commonly known as Altcoins, refer to any digital currencies that do not fall under the category of Bitcoin. Simply put, Altcoins are cryptocurrencies that offer an alternative to Bitcoin.

Altcoins were created in response to the success of Bitcoin, and are often designed to improve upon or offer different features than Bitcoin. Some popular altcoins include Ethereum, Litecoin, Cardano, Bitcoin Cash, Avalanche, Chainlink, and Tether. There are thousands of different Altcoins now.

Altcoins, or alternative cryptocurrencies, differ from Bitcoin in several ways.

Firstly, altcoins often have different features and functionalities than Bitcoin. For example, Ethereum is designed for building decentralized applications and executing smart contracts, while Litecoin is designed for faster and more efficient transactions compared to Bitcoin.

Secondly, altcoins may use different algorithms than Bitcoin for mining and transaction processing. This means that the process of mining and verifying transactions for altcoins can be different than for Bitcoin, and may require different hardware or software.

Thirdly, altcoins may have different maximum supplies than Bitcoin. This means there may be a different number of coins in circulation or available for mining, which can impact their perceived scarcity and value.

Finally, altcoins can have different market capitalizations than Bitcoin. Some altcoins may have a smaller market capitalization than Bitcoin, while others may have a larger market capitalization due to their popularity or use cases.

Overall, altcoins offer a range of unique features and opportunities for investors and traders looking to diversify their cryptocurrency holdings beyond Bitcoin. However, it's important to research and understand the risks and potential rewards of investing in any cryptocurrency before making any decisions.

Chapter 3:
How Cryptocurrency Works

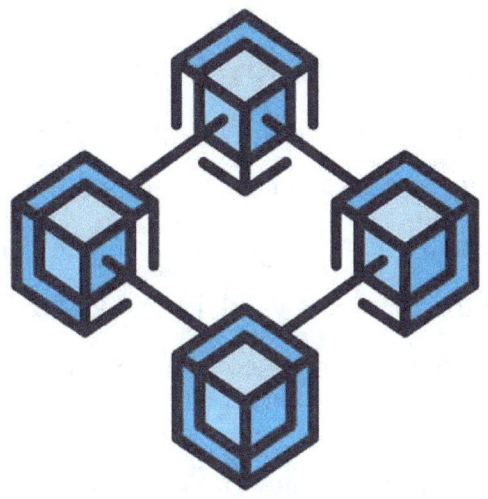

Cryptocurrency & Blockchain

Cryptocurrencies operate on a decentralized blockchain, which is a distributed ledger technology that records all transactions securely and transparently.

The blockchain is maintained by a network of computers, called nodes, that work together to validate transactions and ensure the integrity of the system.

When a person wants to send cryptocurrency to another person, they create a transaction and broadcast it to the network of nodes. Each node on the network checks the transaction to ensure that the sender has enough cryptocurrency to send and that the transaction is valid. If the transaction is valid, it is added to a block of transactions, which is then added to the blockchain.

To ensure the security and integrity of the system, transactions on the blockchain are secured using cryptography. Each transaction is signed with a digital signature, which is a mathematical algorithm that ensures that the transaction can only be modified by the owner of the cryptocurrency.

In addition to recording transactions, the blockchain also serves as a ledger of all previous transactions. This means that anyone can view the entire transaction history of a particular cryptocurrency by looking at the blockchain.

When you own cryptocurrencies, what you own is a private key, which is a secret code that allows you to access your cryptocurrency holdings on the blockchain. This private key is what you store in your digital wallet. I will explain more about wallets later.

How To Send & Receive Cryptocurrencies

When you send or receive cryptocurrencies you use what is called a peer-to-peer transaction.

Peer-to-peer (P2P) transactions refer to the transfer of assets or data directly between two parties without the need for intermediaries like banks or other financial institutions.

In a P2P transaction, the two parties involved interact with each other directly to exchange assets or data, using a decentralized network, such as the blockchain.

The blockchain enables users to transact directly with each other without the need for a centralized authority to verify and process transactions. In a P2P cryptocurrency transaction, the sender and recipient interact directly with each other to exchange cryptocurrency without the need for a bank or other intermediary.

P2P transactions are often faster and cheaper than traditional transactions that involve intermediaries, as there are no fees associated with middlemen. They also offer greater privacy, as the transaction details are not visible to any third parties, and they can be conducted from anywhere in the world with an internet connection.

However, P2P transactions can also carry risks, as there is no centralized authority to oversee and regulate them. Participants need to take appropriate security measures, such as using reputable platforms and verifying the identities of other participants, to avoid fraud and other forms of malicious activity.

The Public Key

In cryptocurrencies, a public key is a string of characters that is used to receive cryptocurrency transactions. It is derived from a cryptographic algorithm and is associated with a specific wallet address on the blockchain.

Then someone wants to send cryptocurrency to your wallet address, they use your public key to create a transaction that sends the cryptocurrency to your address. The public key is shared freely, as it does not reveal any sensitive information about your wallet or cryptocurrency holdings.

The public key is only part of a pair of cryptographic keys used in cryptocurrencies. The other part is the private key, which is kept secret and is used to sign transactions and authorize the transfer of cryptocurrency out of your wallet. The private key is what provides security and control over your cryptocurrency holdings.

The public key is an essential component of the public-key cryptography that underlies cryptocurrencies like Bitcoin. The public-key cryptography system enables secure transactions to be made without the need for intermediaries, such as banks or payment processors, to verify and process transactions.

The Private Key

In cryptocurrencies, a private key is a secret key that is used to sign transactions and authorize the transfer of cryptocurrency out of your wallet. It is derived from a cryptographic algorithm and is associated with a specific wallet address on the blockchain.

When you want to send cryptocurrency from your wallet, you use your private key to sign a transaction that authorizes the transfer of cryptocurrency from your wallet to the recipient's wallet address.

The private key is kept secret and must be protected at all times, as anyone with access to it can authorize the transfer of cryptocurrency out of your wallet.

The private key is only part of a pair of cryptographic keys used in cryptocurrencies. The other part is the public key, which is used to receive cryptocurrency transactions. The public key is shared freely, as it does not reveal any sensitive information about your wallet or cryptocurrency holdings.

The private key is an essential component of the public-key cryptography that underlies cryptocurrencies like Bitcoin.

The public-key cryptography system enables secure transactions to be made without the need for intermediaries, such as banks or payment processors, to verify and process transactions.

Keeping your private key or seed phrase safe is essential for the security of your cryptocurrency holdings. These are the keys that give you access to your funds, so if they fall into the wrong hands, your funds could be stolen.

To keep your private key or seed phrase safe, it is important to store them in a secure location, such as a hardware wallet or a piece of paper kept in a safe place. You should never share your private key or seed phrase with anyone, and you should avoid storing them in digital formats, such as on your computer or in an email. By taking these steps, you can help to ensure that your cryptocurrency holdings remain secure.

Part 2: Buying & Selling Crypto

Buying and selling cryptocurrency is a fundamental aspect of engaging with digital currency. To participate in the cryptocurrency market, you must first obtain some cryptocurrency, which can be done through several methods. Once you have obtained cryptocurrency, you can use it as a long-term investment, purchase goods and services, or sell it for a profit.

Unlike traditional stock markets, the cryptocurrency market operates 24/7 and can be accessed anywhere in the world with an internet connection. Investors can buy and sell cryptocurrency through various methods, such as through cryptocurrency exchanges, and even at cryptocurrency ATMs.

Chapter 4:
Cryptocurrency Wallets

What Is A Wallet

A cryptocurrency wallet is a tool that allows users to, send, and receive cryptocurrencies, such as Bitcoin or Ethereum.

Just like a physical wallet holds cash, a cryptocurrency wallet holds cryptocurrency. However, what is important to understand is that the wallet does not hold your actual coins or assets. The cryptocurrency coins or assets are stored on the blockchain.

Your wallet has two important pieces of information: a public key and a private key.

The public key is like your wallet's address, which you can share with others to receive cryptocurrency. You can think of your public key as your bank account number.

The private key is like a password that allows you to access & move your cryptocurrency to other wallets. You should never share your private key with anyone, as it is the only way to access the cryptocurrency in your wallet. You can think of your private key as your pin for your debit card.

There are two different types of cryptocurrency wallets. Hot wallets and cold wallets are two types of cryptocurrency wallets with different levels of security.

Hot Wallets

A hot wallet is a wallet that is connected to the internet and allows you to access your cryptocurrencies easily and quickly. Hot wallets include software wallets that can be downloaded to your computer or mobile device, as well as online wallets that are hosted by a third party. Hot wallets are convenient to use, but they are also more vulnerable to hacking and theft as they are connected to the internet.

Hot wallets are designed for frequent use, allowing you to quickly access your cryptocurrencies and transact. They are also often free to use and easy to set up.

Hot wallets typically come with a user-friendly interface that allows you to send and receive cryptocurrencies with just a few clicks. Despite their convenience, hot wallets pose a higher risk of being hacked or compromised as they are connected to the internet. Therefore, they are more susceptible to security breaches and theft attempts compared to cold wallets that are kept offline.

It is important to choose a secure hot wallet and take precautions to protect your private keys.

Overall, hot wallets are a convenient way to access cryptocurrencies and make transactions quickly and easily.

However, they are not as secure as cold wallets, which are offline and therefore less vulnerable to hacking and theft attempts.

Software wallets that I suggest & recommend:

Metamask: https://metamask.io

Exodus: https://www.exodus.com

Atomic: https://atomicwallet.io

Klever: https://klever.io

Trust Wallet: https://trustwallet.com

Internet Money Wallet: https://internetmoney.io

Rabby: https://rabby.io

Cold Wallets

A cold wallet is a wallet that is not connected to the internet and is therefore considered more secure than a hot wallet. Cold wallets include hardware wallets that are physical devices, as well as paper wallets that are printed out and stored offline.

Hardware wallets are small, portable devices that allow you to store your private keys offline. They are designed to be tamper-proof and include features such as PIN codes and passphrase protection to prevent unauthorized access.

Hardware wallets typically connect to your computer or mobile device via USB and allow you to make transactions securely.

Hardware wallets that I suggest & recommend:

Ledger: https://www.ledger.com
Trezor: https://trezor.io
Tangem: https://tangem.com
Cypher Rock: https://www.cypherock.com
BC Vault: https://bc-vault.com

Paper wallets, on the other hand, are simply printed copies of your public and private keys that are stored offline. They can be generated using a special software program and are typically printed out on a piece of paper. Paper wallets are free and easy to create, but they are not as secure as hardware wallets as they can be lost, stolen, or damaged.

Cold wallets are commonly used for the long-term storage of cryptocurrencies, as they offer a high level of security and are not vulnerable to online attacks or hacking attempts. They are also a good option for users who cannot access their cryptocurrencies frequently.

However, cold wallets are less convenient to use than hot wallets, as you need to connect them to a computer or mobile device to make transactions.

Combining Both Wallets

Combining a hardware wallet with a software wallet is a common way to achieve both the security of a hardware wallet and the convenience of a software wallet.

To combine the security of a hardware wallet with the convenience of a software wallet, you can use a software wallet that is compatible with your hardware wallet. This allows you to use your hardware wallet to securely store your private keys offline while using a software wallet to make transactions and check your balances.

For example, you can use a hardware wallet like the Ledger Nano S or Trezor to store your private keys offline, and then use a software wallet like Metamask to access your cryptocurrencies and make transactions. You simply connect your hardware wallet to your computer, open the software wallet, and follow the prompts to make transactions.

By combining a hardware wallet with a software wallet, you can have the best of both worlds: the security of a hardware wallet and the convenience of a software wallet.

Restoring A Lost Wallet

If you ever lose your hardware wallet or lose access to your computer with your software wallet, you can always get access to your crypto by restoring your wallet on another device as long as you have your seed phrase. This is why it is very important to keep your seed phrase in a safe place.

Your seed phrase is a series of 12 or 24 random words that are generated when you first set up your cryptocurrency wallet. This phrase is used to restore your wallet in case you lose your device or your wallet becomes inaccessible for any reason.

Restoring your wallet with your seed phrase is a straightforward process. Once your wallet is restored, you will then have access to all of your previously stored cryptocurrencies in your wallet.

It is important to remember that anyone with access to your seed phrase can access your wallet and steal your cryptocurrencies, so make sure to keep your seed phrase safe and secure.

It's also important to note that not all wallets use the same seed phrase format. Some wallets use 12-word seed phrases, while others use 24-word seed phrases. Make sure to check the specific instructions for your wallet before attempting to restore your wallet with your seed phrase.

Chapter 5:
Cryptocurrency Exchanges

Cryptocurrency Exchanges

A cryptocurrency exchange refers to a virtual marketplace where
individuals can purchase, sell, or exchange digital currencies. This
online platform provides users with a convenient and
straightforward means of investing in cryptocurrencies and
accessing various trading options.

It is similar to a stock exchange, but instead of buying and selling stocks, users trade cryptocurrencies like Bitcoin, Ethereum, and many others.

The exchange allows users to create an account, deposit funds, and use those funds to buy or sell cryptocurrencies. Exchanges typically charge fees for transactions, which vary depending on the exchange and the type of transaction.

Some exchanges also offer additional features, such as margin trading and futures trading, which allow users to trade cryptocurrencies with leverage or speculate on future price movements.

It's important to note that not all exchanges are created equal. Some exchanges have more security features and are more trustworthy than others.

It's important to research and compares exchanges before choosing one to use, and always to take precautions to protect your funds and personal information.

Cryptocurrency exchanges that you can check out:

Newton: https://www.newton.co
Coinbase: https://www.coinbase.com
Binance: https://www.binance.com

You can also search Google for an exchange that is available in your country.

Transfer Your Cryptocurrency Off The Exchange

Leaving your cryptocurrency on an exchange can be risky for several reasons:

1. **Hacking:** As mentioned earlier, exchanges can be targeted by hackers who may try to steal funds. If your funds are stored on an exchange, they are potentially vulnerable to such attacks.

2. **Exchange insolvency:** Exchanges can go bankrupt or shut down for various reasons. If this happens, users may lose access to their funds or have difficulty recovering them.

3. **Counterparty risk:** When you hold your cryptocurrency on an exchange, you are effectively trusting the exchange to hold your funds for you. If the exchange engages in fraudulent behavior or mismanages its operations, your funds could be at risk.

4. **Lack of control:** When your cryptocurrency is on an exchange, you may not have full control over it. For example, you may be unable to access it during periods of high demand, or the exchange may limit your ability to withdraw funds.

5. **Regulatory risk:** As mentioned earlier, cryptocurrency regulations can vary by country and change quickly. If a regulatory agency seizes an exchange's funds, your cryptocurrency could be frozen or lost.

To mitigate these risks, it's highly recommended to use a hardware wallet or other cold storage solution to hold your cryptocurrency when not actively trading. This gives you more control over your funds and reduces reliance on third-party exchanges. If you do choose to leave your cryptocurrency on an exchange, be sure to choose a reputable one with strong security measures in place such as using multi-factor authentication to protect your account.

Chapter 6.
The Cryptocurrency ATM

Cryptocurrency ATMs

Cryptocurrency ATMs (Automated Teller Machines) are machines that allow users to buy or sell cryptocurrencies using cash or a debit card.

They are similar to traditional ATMs that dispense fiat currency, but instead, they allow users to interact with the cryptocurrency market.

Using a cryptocurrency ATM is relatively straightforward. First, the user selects the cryptocurrency they want to buy or sell and enters the amount. Then, they insert cash or swipe their debit card and follow the instructions on the screen. The transaction is completed within a few minutes, and the cryptocurrency is transferred to the user's wallet.

There are two main types of cryptocurrency ATMs: one-way and two-way. One-way ATMs allow users to purchase cryptocurrency, but not sell it. Two-way ATMs, on the other hand, allow both buying and selling of cryptocurrencies.

Cryptocurrency ATMs are becoming increasingly popular as people look for convenient and easy ways to buy and sell cryptocurrencies. However, they do come with some risks. For example, the fees charged by cryptocurrency ATMs can be high compared to traditional exchanges.

Additionally, users must carefully choose a reputable ATM operator to avoid scams or fraud. It's also important to note that not all cryptocurrencies may be available for purchase or sale at all ATMs.

Part 3: Privacy & Security in Crypto

Crypto security refers to the measures and protocols put in place to protect your cryptocurrency assets, from unauthorized access, hacking, and theft. Given the decentralized nature of cryptocurrencies, the security mechanisms used to protect them are quite different from those used in traditional financial systems.

If you want to buy & hold your cryptocurrency, take back your freedom, and control your finances; You then essentially become your bank, and you will no longer have the security of the traditional bank. You then will need to take security very seriously.

As quoted from Spiderman:

"With great power comes great responsibility" ~ Uncle Ben, Spiderman

Let's review a few measures that I highly suggest & recommend for protecting your cryptocurrency assets.

Chapter 7.
Malware Protection

Malware Protection

Malware, short for malicious software, is a type of software designed to harm or compromise computer systems and networks.

It can take many forms, such as viruses, worms, Trojans, ransomware, spyware, and adware, and can be spread through email attachments, infected websites, malicious downloads, or even through physical storage devices.

Malware can pose a significant threat to cryptocurrency users, as it can be used to steal private keys, seed phrases, and other sensitive information used to access cryptocurrency wallets.

To protect yourself from malware, use a reputable anti-virus program to scan your computer regularly and detect and remove any malware infections.

I would recommend that you have a good anti-virus or malware protection installed on your computer.

The malware protection service that I use and recommend is Malwarebytes.

The website: https://www.malwarebytes.com

You also want to be cautious of phishing scams. Be cautious of emails, social media messages, or websites that ask for personal information or login credentials. Verify the source and never click on suspicious links.

Chapter 8.
Virtual Private Network

Virtual Private Network (VPN)

A Virtual Private Network (VPN) is a powerful tool that enables users to establish secure, encrypted connections to remote networks over the internet.

This innovative technology provides users with a private and secure browsing experience, shielding their online activities from prying eyes and potential security breaches.

By encrypting user data and rerouting it through secure servers, VPNs offer an extra layer of protection against cyber-attacks, making them a valuable tool for anyone concerned about their online privacy and security.

It can be particularly useful for individuals involved in cryptocurrency due to the potential risks associated with online transactions.

Using a VPN with cryptocurrency can help to increase the security and privacy of your online transactions.

There are several reasons why a VPN can be particularly useful for those involved in cryptocurrency:

1. **Protect your privacy:** When you use a VPN, your internet traffic is encrypted, which means that your online activities are more difficult to monitor or track. This is especially important for individuals involved in cryptocurrency, where even small amounts of information leakage could result in significant financial losses.

2. **Bypass geographic restrictions:** In some countries, access to cryptocurrency exchanges or trading platforms may be restricted or blocked. Using a VPN, you can bypass these restrictions and access these services from anywhere in the world.

3. **Prevent hacking and data breaches:** Cybersecurity threats are a significant concern for cryptocurrency users, as they can result in the loss of funds or sensitive information.

   Using a VPN can help to prevent hacking and data breaches by encrypting your internet traffic and making it more difficult for hackers to intercept or access your online activities.

4. **Increase anonymity:** When you use a VPN, your IP address and location are hidden, which helps to increase anonymity and prevent tracking or surveillance by third parties.

Overall, using a VPN with cryptocurrency can help to increase the security and privacy of your online transactions, and protect you from potential cyber threats.

It is important to choose a reputable VPN provider that offers high levels of security and privacy and to follow best practices when handling your cryptocurrency transactions, such as using strong passwords and enabling two-factor authentication.

The VPN service that I use and recommend is NordVPN.
The website: https://nordvpn.com

Chapter 9.
Two-factor authentication

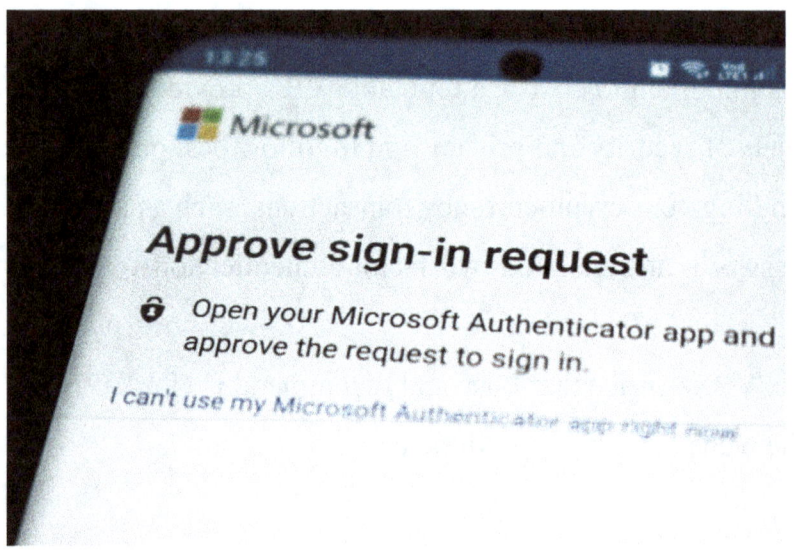

Two-factor authentication (2FA)

To enhance the security of online accounts, many platforms now offer two-factor authentication (2FA) as a vital feature.

In the context of cryptocurrency, 2FA is a recommended security measure to help protect your funds and personal information.

Hackers can gain access to your cryptocurrency account by stealing your password or seed phrase. 2FA helps to prevent this by requiring an additional authentication factor, such as a code generated by an app on your smartphone or a physical token, which makes it much harder for a hacker to gain access to your account.

With 2FA, you receive a unique code every time you attempt to log in to your account. This means that even if someone knows your password, they cannot gain access to your account without also having access to your 2FA device.

It is recommended that you enable 2FA for all of your cryptocurrency accounts and use a reputable 2FA app, such as Google Authenticator or Authy, to generate the authentication codes.

Part 4: Investing Strategies For Crypto

Investing in crypto is not just about buying and holding. Whether you're an experienced investor or a beginner, it is important to have a good understanding of crypto as well as an investment strategy if you want to be profitable.

Chapter 10.
Crypto HODLer vs. Crypto Trader

In the world of crypto, there are two distinct tribes of investors that have emerged. The Crypto HODLers and the Crypto Traders. Each group follows its own strategy. Both groups and strategies for investing in crypto have their own advantages and disadvantages.

Crypto HODLer - The Art of Long-Term Holding

Crypto HODLers are individuals who subscribe to a long-term investment strategy, marked by acquiring cryptocurrencies and retaining them over an extended period. The term "HODL" was born from a humorous misspelling of "hold" in a BitcoinTalk forum post, but it has since evolved into a strategy of buying and steadfastly holding cryptocurrencies, regardless of short-term market turbulence.

The HODLer Advantages

Simplicity and Ease: HODLing is very straightforward. You buy your chosen crypto and patiently wait for it to go up in value over time. No need to be glued to the charts or make snap emotional decisions.

Lower Stress: The crypto markets are known for their rollercoaster-like price swings, which can take a toll on active traders. HODLers, however, can sidestep the stress by ignoring short-term fluctuations and focusing on the potential of their investments in the long run.

Tax Benefits: In many jurisdictions, holding onto cryptocurrencies for an extended period can bring tax advantages, including reduced capital gains tax rates for long-term holdings.

Potential for Substantial Returns: History has shown that many crypto projects have experienced remarkable long-term growth. As a HODLer, you're in it for the long ride, poised to benefit from these upward trends.

The HODLer Disadvantages

Missed Opportunities: The HODLing strategy may cause you to miss out on opportunities to profit from short-term market movements and capitalize on price swings.

Emotional Stress in Bear Markets: During prolonged bear markets, HODLers may experience emotional stress as the value of their investments dwindles significantly, and recovery seems distant.

The Crypto Trader - Actively Trading The Market Ups & Downs

Crypto traders engage in active buying and selling crypto within shorter time frames, leveraging price volatility to generate profits.

Traders use a wide range of strategies, such as day trading, swing trading, and arbitrage, to navigate the crypto market effectively.

Crypto traders are the active participants in the crypto ecosystem. They buy and sell crypto within shorter timeframes, using market volatility to make a profit.

The Crypto Trader Advantage

Profit Potential: Crypto traders have the ability to profit from both the bull market & the bear market.

Skill Development: Trading requires continuous learning and skill development, offering valuable insights into technical analysis, risk management, and market research.

Quick Profits: Traders can capture short-term price fluctuations, potentially yielding quicker returns compared to HODLing.

The Crypto Trader Disadvantage

Higher Risk: Trading crypto carries a much higher risk. A poorly executed trade can lead to substantial losses.

Time-Intensive: Successful trading demands a significant time investment for research, analysis, and market monitoring. It may not be suitable for those with busy schedules.

Emotional Stress: The fast pace of trading can lead to emotional stress, especially during periods of extreme market volatility.

Tax Implications: Frequent trading can result in higher tax liabilities due to capital gains taxes on each transaction.

Choosing between being a Crypto HODLer or a Crypto Trader is a decision that hinges on your financial objectives, risk tolerance, and engagement level with the cryptocurrency market.

Chapter 11.
Managing Your Risk

The crypto market is highly volatile and unpredictable. To protect your investment capital and make informed decisions, you must implement effective risk management strategies.

Crypto investing can be highly volatile and speculative. The prices of cryptocurrencies can experience significant fluctuations in short periods, leading to both substantial gains and significant losses.

This lack of oversight can lead to increased risks of fraud, hacking, and market manipulation.

Avoid FOMO (Fear of Missing Out) Emotional investing can lead to poor choices.

FOMO often plays a significant role and can influence people's decision-making processes.

FOMO is often driven by social pressure and the desire to conform to the behavior of peers or the broader community. When people see others making money or achieving success in a particular investment or activity, they may feel compelled to join in to avoid being left behind.

FOMO can lead to impulsive decision-making, such as buying an asset at a peak price without conducting thorough research or analysis. These iinvestments may result in financial losses if the perceived opportunity turns out to be a speculative bubble or a short-lived trend.

Use hardware wallets or secure software wallets to store your crypto. Keeping your holdings secure reduces the risk of losing your funds to hackers.

The more you understand the assets or activities you're considering, the better equipped you'll be to make informed decisions.

Develop an investment & risk management strategy that aligns with your financial goals and risk tolerance. Stick to your plan, even when FOMO tempts you to deviate.

Chapter 12
Building A Balanced Portfolio

The first thing to consider when it comes to good risk management is building a balanced portfolio of crypto assets.

A balanced portfolio would consist of different cryptos designed to maximize returns while minimizing risk.

For example, you can have your core crypto assets that you have a strong conviction and belief in their potential to be around for the long term, and then you may have another part of your portfolio that you would consider higher risk gamble plays that have a much bigger potential to bring a much higher reward.

Depending on your risk tolerance, your core crypto assets may total 80% - 90% of your entire portfolio. Your higher-risk gamble plays may total 10% to 20% of your entire portfolio.

Some investors may be willing to take on more risk to potentially earn higher returns, while others may prefer to focus on more conservative investments that offer more excellent stability.

It is always a good idea to never invest more than you are willing to lose in any given crypto project.

Invest only money that you can afford to lose without affecting your essential financial obligations.

Spread your investments across different crypto projects to reduce the impact of a potential loss in any one asset.

When building a balanced portfolio you will probably want to keep your portfolio information organized and all in one place. I recommend using portfolio tracking software to keep doing the job of organizing everything.

Tracking and monitoring your crypto portfolio is essential for several reasons, especially given the volatile and rapidly evolving nature of the cryptocurrency market.

Here are a few reasons why tracking and monitoring your crypto portfolio is important:

Well because crazy & insane crypto weirdos like you…. And I have to check and stare at our crypto portfolios at a minimum of 7 times per day. On average, probably 27 times per day, & we need an easy place to go check it.

Financial Awareness and Management: Keeping track of your crypto investments allows you to have a clear understanding of your financial standing. You can see how much you've invested, and the current value of your holdings, and calculate your gains or losses.

This information is crucial for making informed financial decisions and managing your overall investment strategy.

Risk Management: Cryptocurrency markets can be highly volatile, with prices fluctuating dramatically over short periods.

Regularly monitoring your portfolio helps you identify potential risks and adjust your holdings or strategies accordingly.

For example: I often mention that you should have say 1% or 2% in a certain crypto project etc. Well the only way to know how much that is, is if you are tracking your portfolio.

There are many portfolio trackers that you can use to track your crypto assets. Some trackers allow you to connect your wallet so it will automatically sync coins & transactions and then some trackers you will have to manually enter your coins & transactions. Some Trackers and free and some are paid services.

If you have crypto in several wallets and you want to track your crypto in one place you will have to use a tracker where you manually enter all the information. I personally use both types of trackers.

Here is a small list of portfolio trackers that you might consider using. Some of these portfolio trackers allow you to manually enter your coins & transactions as well as connect your wallet to sync transactions.

CoinMarketCap: https://coinmarketcap.com/portfolio-tracker
CoinGecko: https://www.coingecko.com/en/portfolio
DeBank:https://debank.com
CoinStats: https://coinstats.app/portfolio

Chapter 13:
Do Your Research (DYOR)

Do Your Research

Making educated investment selections requires doing your homework before investing in any crypto.

While it could be tempting to buy the newest hype coin or heed the counsel of a well-known influencer, it's important to take the time to investigate the crypto project to understand its basics.

Understanding the Basics

Basics come first on our trip. Take on the role of someone who is learning the language of crypto. Get a good understanding of fundamental ideas like decentralization and blockchain technology to start. You may improve your crypto literacy by starting with books, online courses, and instructional websites.

Project Evaluation

Once you have a solid grounding in the fundamentals, it's time to apply that knowledge to assess specific crypto projects.

Start with the Project's Website

Begin with reading through the website & then read through the whitepaper.

Whitepapers are a great resource for anyone looking to understand a crypto project and make informed decisions.

Here's what you should look for in a whitepaper:

Project Overview: Begin by understanding the project's overarching purpose and vision. What problem does it intend to address?

Use Cases and Utility: Determine the practical applications of the crypto or blockchain technology. How can it be used in the real world? Look for specific examples and scenarios.

Token Information: Understand the role of the native token within the project's ecosystem. Does the token serve as a means of payment, governance, utility, or staking? How is it distributed?

Tokenomics: Analyze the tokenomics, including details on the total supply, initial distribution, token issuance, and any mechanisms for burning or locking tokens. Evaluate whether the token distribution is fair and sustainable.

The Team: Learn about the team members in the project. Review their qualifications and experience in crypto a related field.

Roadmap: Examine the project's roadmap to see its planned development milestones and future objectives. A clear roadmap indicates a well-thought-out strategy.

Explore Official Social Media Channels

X.com (Twitter): Follow the project's official Twitter account for real-time updates and announcements.

Telegram/Discord: Join the project's official Telegram or Discord channels to engage with the community and get insights from discussions.

News Sources

Look into several media and news websites for any current news and partnerships that are being formed.

Google News: Search Google News and see what shows up.

CoinDesk: CoinDesk provides news and analysis on crypto and blockchain technology.

CoinTelegraph: CoinTelegraph is another popular crypto news source with articles on a wide range of topics.

Community and Sentiment

Community is one of the most important factors in crypto. Absolutely.

YouTube: Does the project have a YouTube channel? Also, do a search and see whether there is lots of hype and excitement on YouTube & Twitter about the project. Hype, excitement, and influencers talking about the project are what is going to help the project grow.

Reddit: Subreddits like r/CryptoCurrency and project-specific subreddits can be valuable for discussions and community sentiment.

X.com (Twitter): Search X and get an idea of who and how big the community is for the project.

Crypto Data Websites

CoinMarketCap: Use CoinMarketCap to check the project's market capitalization, price, and historical data.

CoinGecko: CoinGecko provides a comprehensive overview of cryptocurrency projects, including market data, community data, and more.

Technical Analysis

Price Charts: Analyze historical price charts using technical indicators such as moving averages, RSI (Relative Strength Index), MACD (Moving Average Convergence Divergence), and Fibonacci retracements. Look for trends and potential support/resistance levels.

Market Sentiment: Consider market sentiment, as reflected in social media discussions, trading volumes, and order book data. Extreme bullish sentiment can be a sign of overvaluation, while extreme bearish sentiment can indicate undervaluation.

Comparisons with Peers

Relative Value: Compare the project's market capitalization, and other metrics to similar projects in the same sector. If it appears significantly overvalued compared to its peers, it may be overvalued.

Network Activity: Compare network activity metrics, such as daily transactions and active addresses, with similar cryptos. Higher adoption and usage can indicate undervaluation.

Economic Factors

Market Conditions: Consider the overall market conditions and sentiment in the crypto space. Bullish trends often lead to overvaluation, while bearish trends can create undervaluation opportunities.

Global Economic Factors: Keep an eye on global economic events and trends, as they can indirectly affect crypto valuations.

Token Supply and Circulation

Circulating Supply: The number of tokens in circulation affects supply and demand dynamics. A high circulating supply relative to demand may contribute to undervaluation, while a limited supply can lead to overvaluation.

Regularly stay informed by following news and updates related to the crypto project. Developments, partnerships, or regulatory changes can significantly impact valuation.

Remember that the crypto market is highly speculative and sentiment-driven. What may seem undervalued to one investor might appear overvalued to another. Therefore, it's crucial to use a combination of methods, conduct thorough research, and stay informed about market trends to make well-informed decisions.

Chapter 14
Dollar Cost Averaging (DCA)

Dollar Cost Averaging

Dollar Cost Averaging (DCA) is an investment strategy that involves investing a fixed amount of money at regular intervals, regardless of the current price of the assets being invested.

This contrasts with trying to time the market by investing large sums of money simultaneously.

For example, you want to invest $100 in a particular cryptocurrency. Instead of investing the entire amount at once, you could invest $10 weekly over 10 weeks. This way, you will buy the cryptocurrency at different price points over time, potentially reducing the impact of market volatility on your investment.

DCA is a popular investment strategy because it can help to reduce the impact of price volatility on your portfolio. By investing a fixed amount of money at regular intervals, you are buying the asset at different price points, which can help to reduce the impact of short-term market fluctuations.

Another advantage of DCA is that it can help to remove some of the emotional biases that can come with trying to time the market. Instead of trying to predict when the market will rise or fall, you simply invest a fixed amount of money at regular intervals, regardless of market conditions.

Overall, DCA is a simple yet effective investment strategy that can help to reduce risk and improve long-term returns. Investing a fixed amount of money at regular intervals can take advantage of market volatility and potentially build a more robust and profitable investment portfolio over time.

Chapter 15.
Taking Profit Strategies

Taking Profits

Many people in the crypto space adopt the "hodl" strategy, where they hold onto their crypto for the long haul, hoping for substantial price appreciation.

However, even the most steadfast hodlers must know when and how to take profits to protect their investments and realize financial gains.

Create a plan for taking profits. Decide in advance at what price levels or percentage gains you'll consider cashing in your investments. These targets should align with your financial objectives and risk tolerance. Having predefined targets will help you make rational decisions when confronted with the wild price swings typical in the crypto market.

To make the best profit-taking decisions, it is a good idea to often assess your crypto portfolio. Identify assets that have outperformed and that you might consider taking some profits from. A well-managed portfolio is the key to optimizing your gains.

So here are a couple of strategies that you may consider when creating a plan for taking profits in crypto.

Take Partial Profits: Rather than selling your entire position when your profit target is reached, consider taking partial profits. For example, sell 25% or 50% of your holdings to lock in gains while still having exposure to potential future price increases.

Dollar-Cost Averaging (DCA) Out: Instead of selling all your crypto holdings at once, consider a gradual approach. Sell a portion of your holdings at predefined intervals or price levels. This strategy can help you capture gains while potentially benefiting from future price increases.

Keep up with the latest news and developments in the crypto market. External factors like regulatory changes, technological advancements, and market sentiment can all impact the value of your holdings & will also affect your decisions when it comes to taking profits.

Emotions can also play a significant role in your profit-taking decisions. Stick to your predefined strategy and avoid making impulsive decisions based on fear or greed. Trust me, the emotions are real.

Whatever profit-taking strategy you do decide to use, remember to take those profits and secure them in either a stablecoin or back to fiat currency. The crypto market is typically a 4-year cycle and you do not want to hold your bag all the way to the top and then all the way back down to the bottom and then have to wait for the next bull market to come around again.

Chapter 16.
The 4-Year Crypto Market Cycle

The 4-Year Crypto Market Cycle

The "4-Year Crypto Market Cycle" is a concept often associated with the cryptocurrency market, and it refers to a repeating pattern in which significant price movements and market sentiment tend to occur approximately every four years.

This cycle is closely related to the Bitcoin Halving Cycle but extends to the broader cryptocurrency market as a whole.

Here's an overview of the 4-year crypto market cycle:

The Bitcoin Halving Event: This is where everything starts. The Bitcoin Halving often serves as the centre of the entire crypto market cycle. The purpose of the halving mechanism is to gradually reduce the rate of new Bitcoin production until a limit of 21 million is reached. In the following chapter, we will go more into the Bitcoin Halving.

The Bull Run: This is the phase in the crypto market cycle where a sustained increase in the price of crypto, is typically accompanied by high levels of investor optimism and buying activity. Understanding when a bull run starts can be challenging, as it depends on various factors and market dynamics.

Bull runs often begin when market sentiment shifts from bearish (negative) to bullish (positive). Factors such as positive news, favorable developments in the crypto space, and increasing optimism among investors can trigger this shift.

Speculation plays a significant role in crypto bull runs. Traders and investors may enter the market based on the expectation that prices will rise, leading to a self-fulfilling prophecy as increased buying pressure drives prices higher.

Economic conditions, geopolitical events, and monetary policy can influence crypto markets. Factors such as inflation concerns or currency devaluation may drive interest in cryptocurrencies as alternative assets.

Timing the exact beginning of a bull run is challenging, and it often becomes evident only in hindsight. In the past, often we have seen the bull run start within a few months before the Bitcoin halving.

The Crypto Euphoric Parabolic Phase: This is an extreme stage within the crypto market cycle characterized by a rapid, almost vertical, and unsustainable increase in the prices of cryptocurrencies.

This is where the peak of optimism, speculation, and exuberance in the market.
This phase often leads to staggering price gains within a relatively short period.

The most conspicuous feature of the euphoric phase is the skyrocketing prices of cryptocurrencies. Assets that were previously undervalued or overlooked can experience explosive gains over a relatively short period. This sudden price surge can attract significant attention and hype.

FOMO becomes a prevalent emotion during the euphoric phase. Investors, seeing others profit from rising prices, may fear missing out on potential gains. This fear can drive more people to enter the market hastily, often without conducting proper research.

This is where speculation and irrational exuberance are rampant. Investors may buy cryptocurrencies without a clear understanding of their underlying technology or value proposition, driven solely by the expectation of making quick profits.

Optimism reaches irrational levels, with some investors believing that cryptocurrency prices will only continue to rise indefinitely, and traditional financial assets are deemed outdated.

It's crucial to understand that the crypto euphoric phase is inherently speculative and risky. While some investors may profit from buying during this phase, many others may experience significant losses if they buy at inflated prices and the market subsequently experiences a correction or bear market.

This phase only lasts a few weeks or a couple months and usually begins sometime around the end of the bull market.

This is the time when the last of the FOMO investors are rushing into Crypto and the experience investors are taking profits.

The Crypto Bear Market: This is a period in the crypto market characterized by a sustained decline in the prices of cryptocurrencies over an extended period. During a bear market, investor sentiment is generally pessimistic, and there is a lack of confidence in the market's ability to recover quickly.

The sustained and ongoing decline in crypto prices is the most obvious sign of a bear market. This decline may last several months or just a few weeks.

Positive news and developments could be hard to find during a bad market. Negative headlines, security flaws, and regulatory difficulties can all add to the unfavorable mood.

A market correction that leads to a bear market can also come after a period of excessive speculation and unjustified price increases in the euphoric phase.

The Accumulation Phase: This stage of the crypto market cycle is typically regarded as the bottom, or at the very least, close to the bottom of the market due to a period of relatively low prices and decreased trading activity, where shrewd savvy investors gradually accumulated assets. It frequently comes after a bear market or extended period of price decrease and is the first stage of a new market cycle. This phase can often start 6 to 12 months after the euphoric phase, and then last up until a few months before the Bitcoin Halving.

During the accumulation phase, cryptocurrency prices are at or near their lowest points in the cycle. This creates attractive entry points for investors looking to accumulate assets at a discount.

Compared to the previous bear market or the following bull market, volatility tends to be relatively low during the accumulation phase. Prices may still fluctuate, but the extremes seen in earlier stages of the cycle are less common.

Prices may move in a relatively narrow range or exhibit a sideways trend during the accumulation phase. This stability can create a sense of uncertainty and boredom in the market.

The accumulation phase can last for an extended period, ranging from several months to more than a year. It's a time when patient investors focus on building their positions over time. Experienced investors often lead the way during the accumulation phase. The accumulation phase is where the real wealth is made in crypto for those who do the research and take the risk.

It's essential to remember that identifying the precise beginning of the accumulation phase is challenging, and it often becomes evident only in hindsight. Market conditions can vary between cycles, and other external factors can influence the timing and characteristics of this phase.

Although the 4-year cryptocurrency market cycle has shown historical trends, it should be understood that nothing is guaranteed and this does not predict future price changes.

This is crypto, and you can always expect the unexpected.

Chapter 17.
What Is The Bitcoin Halving

The Bitcoin Halving

Few occasions in the dynamic world of cryptocurrencies excite
investors and fans as much as the Bitcoin Halving.

Let's start with the basics: What exactly is the Bitcoin halving?

The Bitcoin protocol has a built-in event called the Bitcoin halving. It plays a crucial role in determining the economics of this innovative digital currency, happening generally every four years. But why is it necessary?

The Purpose of Halving

The Bitcoin halving was designed by, Satoshi Nakamoto, to address two key objectives: Scarcity: Bitcoin was created as a digital alternative to traditional currencies, with a capped supply of 21 million coins.

The halving reduces the amount of new bitcoins created, gradually increasing scarcity.

Incentives for Miners: Bitcoin relies on a decentralized network of miners who validate transactions and secure the network.

Miners are rewarded with newly created bitcoins and transaction fees.

The Mechanics & Process of the Halving

Now, let's get into detail, on how the halving actually works. It's pretty straightforward:

The Bitcoin halving operates on a simple principle: after every 210,000 blocks are mined, the reward for miners is halved. Since a new block is typically added to the blockchain every 10 minutes, this means a halving event occurs approximately every four years.

Here's a historical breakdown:

2009-2012: 50 bitcoins per block.

2012-2016: 25 bitcoins per block (halving occurred).

2016-2020: 12.5 bitcoins per block (halving occurred).

2020-2024: 6.25 bitcoins per block (halving occurred).

2024-2028: Projected to be 3.125 bitcoins per block (expected halving).

The Broader Impact on the Crypto Market

Now, the big question: how does the Bitcoin halving affect the entire crypto market? Here are some insights:

Market Sentiment and Attention: The Bitcoin halving generates immense attention, both within the cryptocurrency community and in the broader media. This heightened awareness can significantly impact overall market sentiment.

Altcoin Correlation: Altcoins, or cryptocurrencies other than Bitcoin, often mirror Bitcoin's price movements during the halving period. This correlation can lead to altcoins experiencing similar price swings.

Volatility: Bitcoin's price is renowned for its volatility, and the halving event can amplify this. Traders and investors may react to the halving news, causing substantial price fluctuations in both Bitcoin and other cryptocurrencies.

Mining Profitability: The reduced block reward post-halving can affect mining profitability. Some miners may leave the network, while others may upgrade their equipment to remain competitive. This dynamic can influence the security and decentralization of the Bitcoin network.

Altcoin Projects: During the halving, investor focus may shift towards Bitcoin as it garners more attention and is perceived as a safer investment. This can temporarily slow down the development and adoption of some altcoin projects.

Chapter 18.
Bitcoin Halving & The Market Cycle

Bitcoin Halving & The Market Cycle

The Bitcoin Halving's Influence on Crypto Market Cycles

What exactly is its relationship with the broader crypto market cycles? In this chapter, we'll unravel the connections between the Bitcoin halving and the ever-evolving crypto market cycles.

Here's how the Bitcoin halving can intersect with the crypto market cycle:

Bull Market Catalyst: In the past, there has been a strong correlation between Bitcoin halving events and the start of new bull markets.

A drop in the rate of new Bitcoin production combined with steady or increasing demand can result in circumstances that increase the price of Bitcoin.

Investors typically have a more positive outlook on the crypto industry as a whole because of this bullish mindset.

Increased Attention: The Bitcoin halving generates significant media coverage and attention within the crypto community.

This increased awareness can attract more participants, including both retail and institutional investors, to the cryptocurrency market.

More participants often lead to increased trading volumes and price volatility, which are characteristic of market cycle peaks.

Altcoin Season: The period following a Bitcoin halving sometimes witnesses what's known as an "altcoin season." Altcoins, which are cryptocurrencies other than Bitcoin, can experience significant price surges as Bitcoin's dominance in the market temporarily diminishes.

This is because some investors look for opportunities in smaller, more volatile coins when Bitcoin's price is perceived as less dynamic.

Post-Halving Corrections: While halving events are generally seen as bullish, the market can also experience significant price corrections following a strong pre-halving rally.

These corrections can lead to a consolidation period or even a bear market for both Bitcoin and the broader crypto market.

Long-Term Implications: Beyond immediate market cycles, Bitcoin halvings have long-term implications for the overall supply dynamics of Bitcoin.

Halvings increase Bitcoin's scarcity by lowering the rate at which new coins are created, which some investors view as a protection against inflation and economic unpredictability.

This long-term story can encourage consistent investment and adoption, affecting market cycles over time.

Miner Behaviour: The network's security and general well-being may be affected by miner behavior as a result of the halving.

Due to lower block rewards, some miners may decide to leave the network or invest in more efficient equipment if mining becomes less economical for them.

Network security and block confirmation times may be impacted by this.

Part 4: Other Things That Are Important

Chapter 19.
Cryptocurrency Taxes

Here are some things a beginner needs to know about taxes in crypto:

Cryptocurrency is taxable: The IRS, The CRA, (or your country's tax authority) treats cryptocurrency as property for tax purposes. This means that buying, selling, trading, and mining cryptocurrencies can result in taxable events.

Taxable events in crypto include selling or trading cryptocurrency for fiat currency (like USD, or CAD), trading one cryptocurrency for another such as selling your Bitcoin & then buying Ethereum, and even using cryptocurrency to purchase goods or services.

It's very important to keep accurate records of all your crypto transactions, including the date, amount, and value in USD at the time of the transaction. This will help you calculate your capital gains and losses accurately.

Taxes in crypto can be complex, so it's a good idea to consult a tax professional who is knowledgeable about cryptocurrency taxation. They can help you navigate the rules and regulations and ensure that you are reporting your crypto transactions accurately.

It's important to note that tax laws and regulations can vary depending on your country or state, so it's important to research and follow the specific rules that apply to you.

You may want to consider using a crypto tax calculator that will help keep track of your portfolio and transactions.

The crypto tax calculator service that I use and recommend is Koinly.

The website: https://koinly.io

Conclusion

In summary, the world of cryptocurrency is a rapidly developing space, with the potential to revolutionize the way we conduct financial transactions.

As this innovative technology continues to evolve, we can anticipate the emergence of new use cases, features, and applications that could transform the world of finance as we know it.

While it has many benefits, such as increased security and privacy, some challenges need to be addressed, such as legal and regulatory issues.

Despite facing several challenges and obstacles, the future of cryptocurrency appears promising. As the demand for decentralized digital currencies continues to rise, we can expect to witness the development of more robust and secure technologies to support their growth. With increasing adoption and mainstream acceptance, the future of cryptocurrencies appears to be vibrant, offering numerous opportunities and possibilities for users and investors alike.

Increased adoption, new use cases, the rise of central bank digital currencies, and technological advancements are all likely to play a role in its development.

As the technology continues to evolve, it is important for users to stay informed and to take steps to protect their cryptocurrency holdings.

By staying informed and taking a proactive approach, we can help to ensure that cryptocurrency realizes its full potential as a safe, secure, and efficient means of conducting financial transactions.

Colin Meunier

decentral21@gmail.com

www.CryptoColin.com